TO

Mary,

Thank you for taking
such care of me on
my recent visit to
the ccu ward,
I hope you find your
"Dream" takes you one
step nearer to your
true Destiny.

with love & God Bless

Patricia Rose Knapton

2002

AKNOWLEDGEMENTS

With gratitude to Hughie Lawrence at United Christian Broadcast (UCB) for writing the foreword for this book, and for making me such a welcome guest on his programme at UCB Europe.

With grateful thanks to Dorothy Mcneil, my publisher, for having faith in me and my writing.

ISBN: 1 872547 87 7

Text: Copyright Patricia Rose Knapton © January 2000

Cover – Illustrations Copyright Gerald Newton © January 2000

Published by Sherbourne Publications
Oswestry, Shropshire SY10 9AG, UK
Telephone/Fax 01691 658753

Typesetting by G. Newton & GM Design, Shrewsbury

Printed by Bookcraft Limited, Bath

Grains of Truth

Thoughts For
The Twenty First Century

Patricia Rose Knapton

Illustrations by Gerald Newton

Sherbourne Publications

This book is dedicated with love and gratitude to my husband, Dave, for his continued love and support.

With special love to our son Paul, his wife Jayne and our granddaughter Rachael. Also to the loving memory of our son, Steven - brother to Paul - forever in our hearts.

To my extended family and wide circle of friends who have also been a source of inspiration.

FOREWORD

After careful consideration, and consultation with my family - Angela, my wife, and my children, Adena, Adeno and Adora - and spending time as a family reading one poem after the other, it struck me that there was a definite unseen inspiration behind every one of these poems; I sensed God in each one. The issues covered ranged from day to day affairs to those of galactical proportions, each one like a present slowly being unwrapped and unravelled to reveal the content. At times we laughed, at other times we were close to tears, but we were always challenged to consider the Creator and to realise that we are just part of a bigger picture.

These poems could easily be read to large gatherings, as well as to small personal settings like ours. Some could be used as the Songs of Solomon were used, to express one's undying love to another, others could be used to compile presentations for varying purposes. Having met Patricia and spent time with her personally, I sense the gentleness and genuineness of her love for people and Creation coming through clearly in each one of her poems. To me every public library and outlet should make this book readily available to as many people as possible.

I think that my words are inadequate to convey the richness of these poems, therefore I recommend a slow methodical read through each one. I am sure, like myself, you will have hours of pleasure.

Hughie Lawrence
Producer/Presenter - UCB Europe
United Christian Broadcast Ltd
Stoke-on-Trent, Staffordshire
ST4 8YY U.K.

December 1999

CONTENTS

CONTENTS

A new *D*awn

A s I stepped out into the breathless morning, a
brilliant sun rose from a cloudless blue sky and I
witnessed the birth of a brand new dawn; the dawn
of a new millennium. Everywhere I looked there was a
stillness as the golden sun bathed the morning in a glow of
peace. Even the birds seemed to utter a sweeter note.

I stood in the quiet beauty of this once in a lifetime dawn
and thought of the people who couldn't be there to see it.
And then I thought of all the joy and love in the hearts of
people, who like myself, felt very privileged to witness
this historic day.

Only hours before, at the stroke of midnight, the whole
world became one huge global party. Millions of people
from all nations thronged the cities and streets, united in
love and peace, to celebrate the birth of a new dawn; the
dawn of peace.

I thought of another time, around two thousand years
ago, when the world celebrated a very special birth. A time
when three wise men brought gifts in celebration of the
birth of a tiny baby; a birth that was destined to change the
world.

We all have gifts we can offer in celebration of the birth
of the millennium, gifts that bear no cost and yet have the
power to change our world; the gifts of Hope, Faith, Love
and Peace.

These are my wishes for you, as you go forward into the
twenty first century.

With much love,

Patricia Rose Knapton
Shrewsbury 2000.

Grains of Truth

There's a whisper going around the mountain,
There's a gentle hush from the breeze,
There's an air of excitement in pastures
And an uplift in the murmuring trees.

There are grains of truth in the cornfields
That the future will look to the past
For nature and man's re-union,
There's an echo of wisdom at last.

There's a breath of fresh air for the songbird
That God's promise will soon be unfurled,
There's a wave of hope in the countryside
For the return to a natural world.

Seeds of Plenty

The many seeds of faith and love
You have sown along the way
Will blossom in abundance
To give you rich rewards one day.

For every single kindly deed
Will come back to you ten-fold;
They may not be counted in silver
And may not be measured by gold.

But you'll gather in your harvest
And be blessed the day you find
You can sow the seeds of plenty
For the good of all mankind.

Harvest of Life

The tide of life is now turning
For the future is given a choice,
Farmers and housewives are about to be heard;
In the past they have not had a voice.

When they can buy bread for the table
Free of genetically modified wheat,
And pick apples free from chemical sprays
That are grown again natural and sweet.

When mothers can feed their young children
Without fears over numbers with 'E'
When water is cleansed over mountain streams
And once again fish can thrive in the sea.

When grace is said around the table
To thank God for the food on the plate,
Food that is grown with love and faith
And when no one need worry over weight.

When man and the soil can work in harmony
With the scythe, the sickle and the sieve,
And return to natural free-range farming
We will go back, to go forward, to live.

A present for the Future

The future is just like a present
Still wrapped in a ribbon of gold,
You may view it with anticipation
For you don't know what it might hold.

There's a sense of mystery and pleasure,
And of happiness it could hold in store,
You look forward with joy and hope it is
Everything you've been praying for.

Though it's exciting to look to the future
The Lord God will help you recall,
The present without the ribbons and bows
Is the most precious gift of all.

The fruits of Your labour

As you stand on the brink of the future
On the eve of a new century,
You can see your dream on the horizon
And all that you wish it could be.

Start by believing in your own worth
And the world will believe in you.
If you have the faith and the courage
You will succeed in all that you do.

Work on an exciting new formula
For achieving your dreams and your goal
Set all of your plans in motion
By giving them your heart and your soul.

Just try to visualise an open stage
Where your dream is in motion now,
And at 'curtain up' you are the star
So be prepared to take your bow.

The world always applauds a winner
So be sure to stake your claim
For all the fruits of your labour
That will bring you fortune and fame.

The Journey

The moment you enter the arrival lounge
Your journey is mapped out for you.
You may be blissfully unaware
But your chosen path will be true.

There will be a great many stepping stones
That will appear to guide your feet
And keep you focused on direction
Until your journey is complete.

There may be pitfalls and disappointments
'Though you will be strengthened by these,
You will see signs that begin to make sense
Of the reason for life's mysteries.

Time is a passage with no clock on the wall
So hurry gently as you rush for success,
The highway of life is a learning curve
That will teach you how to do more with less.

But as long as you have a dream in your heart
With the wisdom to follow it through,
And faith in the road that lies ahead,
Then the future will come to meet you.

You will see the sunrise one morning
Showing all that is meant to be,
And all that is within your gift
Will line the road to your destiny.

A spiritual Eclipse

The final eclipse of the century
Before the millennium,
Meant the world was about to witness
A spectacular phenonemon.

The race was on to the coastline
Where thousands had gathered to view
This once in a lifetime experience,
Now their dream was about to come true.

As millions took to the outdoors
Not a single bird was in flight,
It was a deeply spiritual feeling
And a rare emotional sight.

The shadow of the moon was emerging
Now the total eclipse had begun,
The day was plunged into darkness
As it blotted out the sun.

There was a surge of electrical charges;
A chill on a sudden breeze
And a powerful feeling of unison
With the creator of such mysteries.

As the shadow of the moon passed over,
The sun shone and the world could see,
It was a truly magical experience
That will go down in history.

The colour of Love

If only we could step back in time
And be a child once more,
When the air was as pure as laughter
And trust was on sale in each store.

When love was a friend in a classroom
Regardless of colour or race,
When innocent hearts without prejudice
Had faith in a smile on a face.

When the future was coloured in sunshine
And there was never a dark cloud above,
When they painted a world of God's children
They saw only the colour of love.

In the Palm of Our hands

There is a mist on the horizon
At the turn of the new century,
One is slowly coming to a close
While the next is yet to be.

There is an air of expectation
As we sail uncharted seas,
There is a hint of trepidation
About wars, famine and disease.

But all who believe in Lord Jesus
Will approach it with joy in their heart
For they will all know of God's promise
And so will have faith from the start.

It is the start of all new beginnings
A chance for the planet's re-birth,
A time to redress the balance
And give back all we took from the earth.

It's the beginning of a promising new era
Where impossible dreams will come true,
It's a chance to turn our world around
From an inspirational point of view.

For each of us holds the future
In the palm of our hands in prayer,
For God has the power to heal the world
And all its people everywhere.

The firethorn
And the blackbird

The Firethorn's winter berries
Are designed to catch the eye
Of any hungry blackbird
That may be passing by.

It may seem to those who witness it
The blackbird devours them with greed,
But the Firethorn knows it's a perfect way
To propagate its seed.

The giving and taking in nature
Has worked well for centuries;
The bees rely on the flowers
And the flowers rely on the bees.

And if man can follow nature's lead
Where give and take comes naturally,
Like the Firethorn and the blackbird
He will live in harmony.

A *new* D*irection*

When you come to a major crossroads
In your life and it's hard to know
Which of the signposts to follow
And just which way you should go.

Take the road with the signpost 'for you'
A road that will lead you to love,
Follow it through with trust in your heart
And faith in the good Lord above.

But should you get lost on life's highway
And fear you'll end up in despair,
Try asking God for directions
At the heart of a quiet prayer.

Take hold of his hand on your journey
Let him guide every step to your goal,
He will give you a brand new direction
To embrace with your heart and soul.

*W*ho makes *R*ainbow?
the

Who paints the colour in a sunset's glow
And who sets the diamonds that shimmer on snow?
Who gives the stars their brilliant light
And who lights the moon that shines at night?

Who gives the tide its ebb and its flow
And who gives the wind the whistle to blow?
Who makes a rainbow from sunshine and showers
And who makes the roses such beautiful flowers?

Who makes the sun rise and then set
And who guides the boats and the fishing net?
Who gives the eagle its powerful wings
And who gives the songbird its song to sing?

Who gives the earth the air that we breathe
And who gives us hope and faith to believe?
Who gives all this with unconditional love?
Almighty God in heaven above.

If you have
Love for your world

If you have love for your neighbour
You will live in peace.

If you have love for your garden
You will tend it with pride.

If you have love for your family
You will cherish them always.

If you have love for your animals
You will protect them with compassion.

If you have love for the countryside
You will try to keep it tidy.

If you have love for your food
You will grow it naturally.

If you have love for your rivers
You will cut down on waste.

If you have love for your forests
You will cut down on wood.

If you have love for your world
You can change it....with love.

13

To live the *Dream*

Oh to rest by a quiet stream
In the morning sun to dream a dream.
With time to watch a rabbit on the run
And a kestrel's wings eclipse the sun,
Then dip and lift on a thermal glide
As its shadow crosses the mountainside.
Where the silence echoes the mystery
Of why the spirit can feel what the eyes cannot see;

Dry parchment fields bereft of grain
Now lush and gold and green again.
And a sunburst over the hills of hope
For the forest deer and the antelope,
And crystal streams run down the mountainside
Where the lion and the lamb lie side by side.
Oh to rest and dream beside the healing spring
To dream the life....and to live the dream.

Every moment Counts

What good is striving
For all the trappings of wealth,
Working every hour God sends
At the expense of one's own health.

What good is striving
To be always the perfectionist,
Setting standards far too high
So that a 'day off' doesn't exist.

What good is striving
For the top of the business tree,
When it robs you of precious time
To spend with your family.

What good is striving
To make time in retirement account
For all the time spent wishing
You had made every moment count.

*B*lind *F*aith

A person may open the curtain,
Look out of the window
In the middle of the night
And see only the darkness.

But a blind person may open the curtain,
Look out of the window
In the middle of the night
And see only the light.

For they possess the gift
Of blind faith

A heavenly Waveband

You will need to be connected
To find the right frequency
Before you select the channel
Where the airwaves are for free.

Then open up your heartline
And tune into a prayer,
Turn to the heavenly waveband
And you'll find that God is there.

You will get a great reception
From the host on high above
Once you are in tune with God
You'll be receiving all his love.

The first Step

A man may have
Climbed the highest mountain,
Sailed the seven seas,
Travelled the world
And walked on the moon.

And yet may not have
Even begun his travels,
For his long journey starts
With the first step
Of the first mile...
With the lord.

If we truly Believe

I've never seen God
But I truly believe.
I can't see the air
But I know that I breathe.

I can't hold the air
In the palm of my hand;
It's invisible, intangible
And hard to understand.

But it's true we need God
As much as the air we breathe,
And we can all feel his love
If.....we truly believe.

The Innocents

They come in their thousands
Through storm laden skies,
Fractured young families
With despair in their eyes.

They come with their memories
Of torture and rape,
Of horrors so gruesome
They cannot escape.

Forced from their homes
By the butt of a gun,
In the name of God
They ask, 'What have we done?'

The villages they loved
No longer exist,
They are homeless and helpless;
Just a name on a list.

Where are the husbands
The fathers and sons?
The old and the feeble
And the innocent ones?

A sea of lost souls
Awash without hope,
Who fear for their future
When their neighbours can't cope.

Pitiful messages
Windswept on a wall,
Searching for loved ones
When there's no news at all.

From a tent in a mudfield
A new baby cries,
Born without prejudice
In a war it defies.

What kind of madness
Is fuelled by greed
In the mind of a tyrant
Who will never succeed.

For the children will Sing
A new song of peace,
Uniting all nations
So all wars will cease.

A cross to *B*ear

Everyone has a cross to bear
As they travel along life's road,
Some may be light to carry
But some are a heavy load.

They come in different sizes
And some may be measured by fears,
Some may be lifted in hours
But some may feel heavy for years.

Some may be fashioned by heartache
And some may be loaded with pain,
Some may be carried in sunshine
And some may be carried in rain.

As you struggle along life's highway
The good Lord will help you recall.
The one that's carried with love in the heart
Is the cross that's the lightest of all.

*T*rust *H*im

When it's so hard to lift the veil
That seems to cloud your view
And you just can't face that open road
That looms ahead of you;

When 'moving on' is a stumbling block
Where hope gives way to fears,
When your heart is crying out for love
And your eyes fill with lonely tears.

Try to seek out a quiet place
Where you have the time to pray
And open up your heart to God
His love will show you the way.

Trust him with your heart and soul
When it's the hardest thing to do,
Put your faith and trust in God
And his love will help you through.

*E*arthly *A*ngels

When we think of an angel
We think of heavenly wings
Floating on a distant cloud
With a voice that softly sings.

But there are many angels
Who we often daily meet,
They may just be passing by
On some crowded city street.

One may see you struggling
With a heavy shopping load
And offer you a helping hand
As you walk along the road.

Or when you ask for directions
At a point where you feel lost,
One may say, "I'll take you there"
With a smile that says "no cost".

Or one may have a loving hand
That reaches out to give
A crust of bread to a hungry soul
And the precious will to live.

There are many earthly angels
We may meet them unawares,
But when you see one you will know
That someone truly cares.

A living Saint

Her's were the hands of an angel
Though her face was furrowed with age,
And if we could have read between the lines
There was a story to tell on each page.

She devoted her life to the needy
Finding food for the young and the old,
The hungry, the weak and the feeble,
With a heart that was made of pure gold.

She walked among thousands of starving
As she tended the injured and lame,
She held hands with the sick and the dying
And prayed for their souls in God's name.

She nurtured a team of young angels
While working exhausted herself,
Feeding their souls with compassion
When there was no more bread on the shelf.

She gave her life and her love without question
Not looking for praise or a prize,
She will be remembered as a living saint
Now and forever in people's eyes.

She has passed every exam for the living
With a degree of distinction in love,
And has gained a place reserved only for saints
On high up in Heaven above.

The door will Open

There are times when happy memories
Can be painful to recall
And it may seem that they desert you
When you need them most of all....

Like a door that gives you just a glimpse
As it stands invitingly ajar,
Where all your beautiful memories seem
So very near and yet so far....

But time will gently open wide
Your precious 'memory' door
Giving you back your happy memories
To cherish for ever more.

The longest Sleep

Death is but a kiss goodnight
In peaceful sleep it dims the light
As it slips into the longest sleep
It has no clock or time to keep.

Death is but a veil of peace
When all that was has come to cease.
It feels no pain, no sting of tears,
No sense of loss for stolen years.

Death is but a star at night
In darkest hours it shines a light.
It gives the Lord its soul to keep
While it sleeps the sleep of the longest sleep.

Beyond the Blue

Life is like a butterfly
That spends its life earthbound,
With a caterpillar overcoat
Until the time comes around;

To shed its heavy mantle
And emerge with gossamer wings
In a golden shaft of sunlight
Where a far away angel sings.

In this glorious transformation
Death holds no mystery,
For the butterfly, like the spirit,
Was born to fly and be free.

It lifts its wings and flies skyward
Out of reach and out of view,
Towards a place called Heaven
Somewhere beyond the blue.

The flight of the Spirit

The spirit can fly
At the speed of light
Across the world
Of dreams at night.

It can take you far
To reach your goal
With a strength to lift
Your heart and soul.

The spirit can feel
What the eyes cannot see
It can travel through time
And in memory.

The spirit can cross
The great divide
And meet the soul
On the other side.

For the spirit transcends
The earth and the sea;
The moon and the stars
And infinity.

The spirit can rest
In heaven above
And yet still it can fly
On the wings of love.

Hold On

When you go through a tunnel of darkness
And you think it will never end,
When you search for the light of comfort
And the caring support of a friend.

When it seems these all desert you
And you're struggling to make it through,
Take hold of God's hand on your journey
And his light will come shining through.

Terms of Enlightenment

When a loved one dies
We say we have *lost* them,
But they are not lost
They are found...in us.

When a loved one dies
We say they have *died*,
But they are still living,
Living ... in spirit.

When a loved one dies
We say our life is *empty*
But life is not empty
It is still full...of memories.

Quiet Ways

I find my God in quiet ways,
In the peaceful evening skies.
In the silence of an empty church,
And in smiling children's eyes.

I find him in a summer rose,
In a fragrant perfumed breeze.
I find him in a nest of birds,
In a sunburst through the trees.

I find him in a rainbow's arc,
In sunshine and in rain.
I find him in my garden,
And in a field of golden grain.

I find him in a stranger;
By a smile we are apart.
But most of all I find him
In the quiet of my heart.

Food for Your soul

When the cupboard of life runs empty
And your heart is fresh out of love,
And pressure has made holes in your pockets
Depressing those dark clouds above.

If you've searched for a friend in a bottle
And pinned all your hopes on a star,
When you've reached the end of your journey
And you've lost sight of just who you are.

God is the best friend you can turn to
When you fear you can no longer cope,
For he has the power to answer prayers
And renew your spirit with hope.

For the good Lord will never judge you
And if you ask him in a quiet prayer,
He will give you food for your soul
And more than enough love to share.

A lamp to *Y*our feet

Let the good Lord guide you
And be like a lamp to your feet.
Take his hand as you travel
Along the path of any street.

Shine your light for others
So they may clearly see
That they are not alone,
God's love shines constantly.

Spread the light of comfort
Everywhere you go,
And shine your light in darkness
For an everlasting glow.

A sign of hope *F*or the future

When Jesus died for you and me
Upon a cross on Calvary,
God the Father called his Son above
And the world witnessed the greatest love;

The day grew dark
The wind blew strong,
The lightning flashed
And there was no bird song.

In nineteen hundred and ninety nine
The world grew restless for a sign,
As the moon eclipsed the sun on high
There was a powerful spiritual feeling nigh;

The day grew dark
The wind blew strong,
The lighting flashed
And there was no bird song.

Perhaps a sign of hope for the future
That a new dawn has begun,
In spiritual proximity
With God the Father and the Son.

God is Love

Who is God?
It is hard to define
Someone as loving
And as truly divine.

What is love?
It is hard to define
Something as beautiful
And as truly divine.

God is love
And it is easy to define
When we feel his love
It is truly divine.

A compassionate *F*riend

When you need someone to talk to
Who will reach out and hold your hand,
And to know that when they listen
They will truly understand.

When you need a cup of kindness
Before the tears begin to fall,
And a heart full of compassion
To help you through it all.

When you need to know that someone
Knows exactly how you feel,
Someone who identifies
And who knows your pain is real.

When you need to open up your heart
To find you are on the mend,
You need to know you can reach out
To a kind and compassionate friend.

A cup of *Love*

No one need ever be lonely
Downhearted or just feeling bored,
There is always someone to turn to
For you have a friend in the Lord.

He will meet you in a quiet prayer
Where you can share a cup of love,
You can tell him all your troubles
And those clouds will melt above.

He will listen to your problems
And soothe away your fears,
He will lift your heart with his love
And wipe away your tears.

When your cup of love runs over
And you've shared a few more prayers,
You will feel God's hand in yours
And will know he truly cares.

He's a friend you can always rely on
To love you and see you through,
And he is the only friend I know
Who will always be there for you.

*I*nfinity

There are as many stars
Out of reach
As there are grains of sand
Upon the beach.

So when you look up
At the galaxy
You begin to glimpse
Infinity.

If you look beyond
You just might
See God's love
Is infinite.

A quiet Prayer garden

Many people will have a garden
With a quiet corner to spare,
Somewhere they can be alone
To talk to God in prayer.

A little rustic wooden seat
Beneath an overhanging tree,
Some flowers and a little peace
Is all there needs to be.

A place to call your sanctuary
Away from the ringing phone,
Somewhere you can always be
At one with God alone.

But if you have no garden
With a quiet corner to spare,
Try to think yourself a garden
Where you can go in quiet prayer.

A prayer garden within the mind
Can be a rhapsody of rose,
Around a sunshine seat and a waterfall
Where spiritual ambience flows.

$D^{ear}L^{ord}$

Dear Lord,
We need Jesus now more than ever;

For the blind
Who have lost sight of their vision,
For the deaf
Who have closed their ears to the wise,
For the hungry
Who are starving for spiritual guidance,
For the thirsty
Who thirst for the cup of plenty,
For the sick
Who have lost faith in miracles,
For the bereaved
Who are searching for answers,
For the abandoned
Who have lost all sense of hope,
For the world
That is crying on life's shoulder.

Yes Lord,
We need Jesus now more than ever.

My prayer For you

I said a prayer in the quiet of night
That you would find the strength to fight
The battle you've tried hard to win,
And to feel a ray of hope within.

I prayed the healing had begun,
That you'd soon feel the kiss of sun
Upon your cheeks once more again
Free from all life's worry and pain.

To feel the breeze tousle your hair
And lift your heart without a care,
To face the day and feel complete
Once more to know that life is sweet.

I asked not for any measure of wealth,
Only for the priceless gift of health.
I prayed for you because I care
And I believe God heard my prayer.

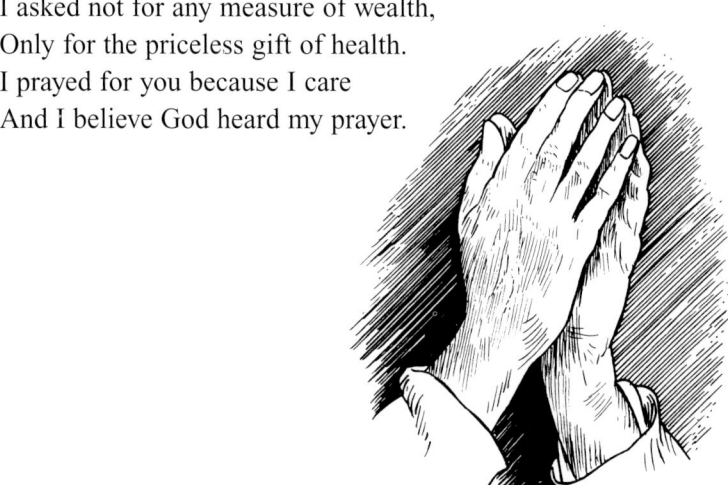

The greatest Friend

At times your home may be cluttered
And you pray no one will call
To find you haven't done your chores
Because you've had no time at all.

But a true friend will never notice
If you have not tidied through,
A true friend will only ever call
To see the friend in you.

And God will never notice
If your home or dress isn't smart,
No matter if you are rich or poor
He only sees your heart.

*F*aith in *L*ove

You cannot see it in your heart
But you know when it is there.
You can give it and receive it
And it's something you can share.

It can lift you up and bring you down
And it can turn your world around.
It can join two hearts together
And can be lost and can be found.

You cannot see it or touch it
It can neither be bought or sold.
It cannot be saved or measured
And is never young and never old.

You can't describe it only feel it
Like one's faith in God above,
But once you feel it in your heart
You will know that God is love.

The heart of a Diamond

If you have a dream that is special
But determination goes astray
Because it seems at every turn
Some obstacle blocks your way.

There may be a very good reason
But only the good Lord above
Knows there are many lessons to learn
Like endurance and faith in his love.

A patient heart is a blessing
If you can't yet cross over the stream,
Life's knocks are there to shape and shine
All the edges of your dream.

For a bright and precious diamond
Is a stone that's cut roughly at the start
And it may take many cuts of the chisel
Before all its facets reflect from the heart.

So hold on to your precious dream
And when the time is right for you,
Just like the heart of a diamond
Your brilliance will come shining through.

*W*ise is the *C*hild

The hands of time can move slowly
For bones that are stiffened by age,
But there is always a wealth of wisdom
In the willing voice of a sage.

Her frame may be weak and weary
But her wisdom is golden and strong,
Her heart holds the book of knowledge
And she is happy to pass it along.

For youth is the child of learning
And wisdom the parent of time,
If youth has the patience to listen
The reason will give them a rhyme.

Wise is the child that learns to respect
The wisdom that's gained from the sage,
When life is the signpost to learning
And experience the Mother of age.

Your true Value

Everyone is someone
So be proud of yourself,
When you get up in the morning
Don't leave your worth upon the shelf.

Dress yourself in confidence
And remember to wear a smile,
Put your best foot forward
Then face the world in style.

Remember the value you put on yourself
Is the price that someone will pay
To get to know and love you
Because you are someone special today.

Rose of Love

My doorbell rang with roses
But just the fragrance was for me,
A card within the foliage read
'In Loving Memory'

My mind rolled back the pages
Of a book too sad to lend,
It was written with a heartache
And with sorrow had to end.

I placed a rose for loneliness
By a rose for a broken heart,
I placed a rose for bitterness
By a rose we are apart.

I placed a rose so full of love
By a rose for happy years,
I arranged them all with misty eyes
And watered them with tears.

I felt the sunshine walk beside me
Once a lonely week had passed,
All around there was a gentle peace
Although the roses didn't last.

But there amongst the embers
Was a rose still fresh with dew,
That single rose lives on today
My rose of love so true.

God spoke to me with roses
And now the tears are gone
From my bouquet of emotions
Just the rose of love lives on.

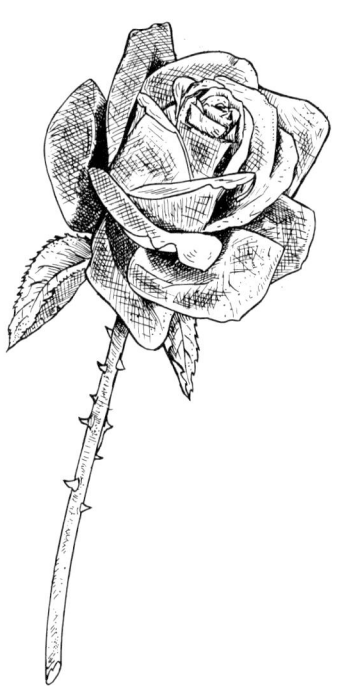

*B*oth sides *of* *T*he mirror

A compassionate heart is priceless
To someone who is recently bereaved,
But some people may cross the road
Afraid of how they'll be received.

Their heart may be a two-sided mirror
Reflecting the pain they can see,
While deflecting their innermost fears
For their own mortality.

But life's rocks are the very foundation
On which friends and most family trees,
Are built to withstand all emotions
That accompany adversities.

It's true, the heart that feels compassion,
For the grief in another's eye,
Is closer to God in that moment
Than the heart that just walks on by.

Light and Shade

When you're waking from darkness
How wonderful it is to see
The sun light up the morning
With its peace and tranquillity.

When you're walking in the shadows
On a bright and sunny day,
Remember sunshine makes the shadows
You may find along life's way.

When your heart is full of sorrow
It's because you've known what it is to love.
Through winter comes the joy of spring
Which is a blessing from above.

Sometimes it helps us to understand
That our suffering is never in vain,
If we're to grow and blossom like the flowers
We need the sunshine and the rain.

*R*eflections of *A* swan

Have you ever stopped to watch
A swan upon the lake?
And have you ever marvelled,
In the moment it will take.

How gracefully it glides along
With its regal head held high,
So serene and elegant
While the world just passes by.

Yet underneath this air of grace
As you watch it gently pass,
Is a pair of feet treading water
Like a drum in a heart of glass.

Some people are just like the swan
Who on the surface glide,
And look serene to all the world
Yet can be crying deep inside.

*W*here there *I*s hope

If you are struggling around the shops
To buy a suitable card that you could
Send to someone who is very ill;
Perhaps the prognosis isn't good.

If you are searching for a 'Get Well' card
That doesn't exactly say 'Get Well'
And you've tried so hard to find a card
With a message the shops don't sell.

Try casting aside your own fears
Even though it may be hard,
Think of all you would wish yourself
And then buy them a 'Get Well' card.

For they will read between the lines
Of a card that does not say
'Get Well Soon' for we all need hope
And to know hope is on its way.

*M*oving *O*n

As we travel through life's thoroughfare
It's often hard to keep in touch
With all those friends along the way
Who have meant so very much.

But life has many stepping stones
All designed for moving on,
And often when you are looking back
You find they have moved or 'gone'.

But if your smile has touched their heart
And perhaps you've lent a helping hand,
Or given them your precious time
And have said you understand.

If you've made a difference to their lives
And made the sun shine on their day,
You will forever be remembered
In a very special way.

A *quiet* *R*oom

There is something very peaceful
About a darkened room at night
That is lit by just a candle
And the soft glow of firelight.

With curtains drawn in a quiet room
Against the sound of the rain,
There's a sense of peace all around
As it drums on the window pane.

Where a flickering candle beckons
To a book with an open page
And beside it stands a glass of wine
That has seasoned well with age.

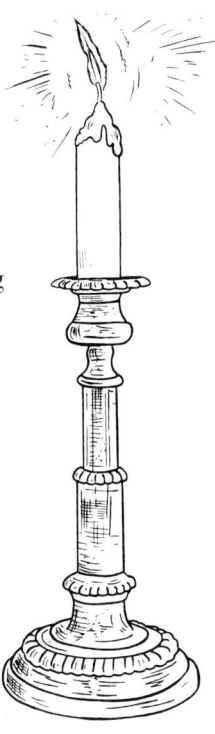

Where there's a gentle sound of ticking
From a clock on the mantle shelf,
That's the perfect time in a quiet room
To find the peace within yourself.

Trophies of The heart

Don't be afraid of a challenge
No matter how daunted your nerve
And don't be discouraged by failure,
For life is a long learning curve.

Success isn't always about winning,
It comes from just taking part.
When you've found your strength and courage
The trophies will be all in your heart.

If you have A dream

Love is the glow on your horizon
Hope is the Spring in your heart,
Faith is the key to believing
Success can be yours from the start.

If you have a dream in the making
And a positive mind, it is true
Nothing for you is impossible,
You can make dreams come true.

A second *C*hance

If you've tried yet somehow failed
To reach the height you thought you'd scaled,
Don't let *fail* become a word
That loses hope each time it's heard.

Be determined to take a stance
For you're entitled to a second chance.
There is always one more avenue
That faith will find just right for you.

So stake your claim, affirm your right
To try again and you just might
Find a star that you can pin
All your dreams upon and win.

Aim for the goal within your eyes
And when the time is right you'll win the prize.

Take Time

Take time to smell the roses
And to linger for a while
Among the peaceful flowers
To give your heart a smile.

Take time to feel compassion
For the grief in a stranger's eye,
Or to call on a housebound neighbour
As you are passing by.

Take time to walk along a lane
Where banks of primroses slope,
To know they've made it through the snow
Will fill your heart with hope.

Take time to watch the sunrise
Bring the morning fresh awake,
And take time to count your blessings
While time is yours to take.

*P*eace of *M*ind

True happiness is found
In the happiness you give
As you travel through life's thoroughfare.

And comfort is found
In the comfort you give
When you are showing someone you care.

But healing is found
In the answer you seek
Of the question that leads you to find

The path to the God-given treasure…
The peace of a quiet mind.

*B*rickbats and *B*ouquets

A harsh word said in anger
Is like a brickbat to the heart,
It can often hurt deep inside
And from memory never part.

But a kind word said in earnest
Can be one of life's bouquets,
It can put the sunshine in a smile
On the rainiest of days.

It is hard to hand out brickbats
Once you've found in many ways
The joy of being the recipient
Of one of life's bouquets.

What does it take To give

What does it take to give generously
When you have so little to spend,
What does it take to give someone a hug
When you see they're in need of a friend.

What does it take to give someone a smile
Whose spirit is downcast and low,
What does it take to give someone praise
When their heart is in need of a glow.

What does it take to give someone hope
When their eyes are full of despair,
What does it take to give someone a hand
And to let them know that you care.

What does it take to give someone faith
To believe in themselves from the start,
What does it take to give so much love?
It takes a bounteous giving heart.

*T*he voice *of T*omorrow

Children are born free of prejudice
Just an innocent trust in their eyes,
With a beautiful dream in the making
And not a single cloud in their skies.

Children will never go hungry
If they are fed with a heart full of love,
With plenty of hope and food for the soul
And faith in the good Lord above.

If they're dressed in a coat of confidence
And are given a voice to be heard,
They will become the teachers
And one day will have the last word.

For the children are the voice of tomorrow
And if nurtured today to make plans
To take great care of tomorrow's world
Then our future will be in safe hands.

OTHER BOOKS BY PATRICIA ROSE KNAPTON

INSPIRATIONAL VERSES

(Gift packed)	ISBN	RRP	
Tapestry of Verse	1 872547 62 1	£2.85	p/b
Curtain of Faith	1 872547 67 2	£2.85	p/b
Garden of the Heart	1 872547 57 5	£2.85	p/b

	ISBN	RRP	
Bella - *the story of a famous guide dog*	1 872547 96 6	£4.45	p/b

All of the above books or additional copies of this book, can be purchased by mail order direct from the publisher, Sherbourne Publications, Trefonen Road, Morda, Oswestry, Shropshire SY10 9AG.

Please enclose cheque with order. P&P 75p per book, or £2.50 all four. Cheques to be made payable to Sherbourne Publications.

For catalogue please write, first or second class stamp for return appreciated.